WHERE'S MY BUCKET AND SPADE?

MEMOIRS OF AN AMATEUR ARCHAEOLOGIST

Dr PAMELA DAVENPORT

Where's My Bucket and Spade?
Memoirs of an Amateur Archaeologist

First published in Australia by Dr Pamela Davenport 2024

Copyright © Dr Pamela Davenport 2024
All Rights Reserved

*A catalogue record for this
book is available from the
National Library of Australia*

ISBN: 9780975112946 (pbk)
ISBN: 9780975112953 (ebk)

Typesetting and design by Publicious Book Publishing
Published in collaboration with Publicious Book Publishing
www.publicious.com.au

No part of this book may be reproduced in any form,
by photocopying or by any electronic or mechanical
means, including information storage or retrieval
systems, without permission in writing from both the
copyright owner and the publisher of this book.

To my wonderful parents Eric and Winifred, and all the family, friends, teachers, and students, who have journeyed with me.

Contents

Acknowledgements i
Foreword iii

Chapter 1 – A dream come true 1
Chapter 2 – The island of Aphrodite 3
Chapter 3 – Mending my first pot 7
Chapter 4 – A pleasant routine 13
Chapter 5 – Ancient discoveries 15
Chapter 6 – My life in ruins 19
Chapter 7 – Reading the ruins 22
Chapter 8 – Exploring Paphos and Kourion 25
Chapter 9 – Cypriot hospitality over
               the Troodos Mountains 31
Chapter 10 – The Customs House and first farewell 37
Chapter 11 – The lifting of the Mosaic of Orpheus 40
Chapter 12 – Uncovering unguentaria and skeletons 50
Chapter 13 – More Cypriot hospitality 55
Chapter 14 – The Mosaics 60
Chapter 15 – A short winter visit to Cyprus 63
Chapter 16 – Stories amongst the sherds 65
Chapter 17 – Yeroskipou, Aphrodite's sacred gardens 71

Illustrations 77

Acknowledgements

I would like to acknowledge the invaluable contributions to this book of many good friends, family, neighbours and nurses who helped me with the arduous task of farewelling my Brisbane home of 60 years while finishing this book.

My 'editing team' who stepped in to assist with finishing the book while I have been unwell: Anne Young, Gaye Pitman, Julianne Deeb and Genevieve Johnston (daughter of Anne). Anne is my oldest school friend, Gaye, a friend and colleague also attended my Greek tours and Julianne is a fellow amateur archaeologist featured in this book, all with a school connection.

I also extend my gratitude to Heather Swatherly and Dennis Roussounis, who assisted with my manuscripts and photos; and to Geoff Ginn, who drew the beautiful illustrations, somehow capturing the magic of Cyprus. This is his second book partnership with me in two years. I would also like to express my sincere gratitude to my agent, Alex Adsett.

Finally and most notably, to my long-time Cypriot friend and colleague, Dr Demetrios Michaelides, Emeritus Professor of Classical Archaeology, University of Cyprus, and his wife Sarah Lee, who took me under their wings in Cyprus. Demetri's expertise accompanied my travels, he generously clarified many technical points and provided descriptions; Demetri and Sarah personify Cypriot hospitality, and our long friendship is inextricably linked to my personal archaeological journey.

Thank you all.
Pamela Davenport

Foreword

This book is testament to Pam's indomitable spirit. All who know and love Pam recognise her powerful intelligence, determination and energy. And we are drawn to her sense of adventure, curiosity and her love of mankind (including animals).

I am one of Pam's many former students; we number hundreds or perhaps thousands and are profoundly grateful for the great good fortune of having been under her tutelage. In Pam's class, my own love of history was forged and my determination to study classics and ancient history firmly set. As a new graduate, I was lucky to be able to join Pam for a season of digging in Paphos and to bring my friend Andrea Rowe, who went on to specialise in Cypriot archaeology and attain a PhD in bronze age pottery. My parents joined Pam on her tours through the Mediterranean and mum shared Pam's love of history, languages and travel. They had been at school together, though in different years and shared happy memories of studying Arts at the University of Queensland and working at the State Library of Queensland. I still love hearing Pam recalling the stories of those days, especially of my father waiting for mum to finish work at the library in their courting days.

Pam has been a part of my life for most of my life, so it is a delight and privilege to introduce this, her third book. It is a vivid recollection of Pam's happy memories in Cyprus and serves as a great reminder to follow your passion, wherever it leads. Though my own path led away from studying archaeology my fascination with the subject abides, as is the case for many in Pam's orbit.

This book brings together Pam's loves of learning, teaching, history, archaeology, academia, travel, Cyprus and most importantly sharing all this with others – as the perpetual and generous teacher she is. In preparation for the book, I had a wonderful time reading Pamela's travel diaries with her, remembering details of the events from 35 years ago. Though her eyes were failing, her memory is crisp. We consulted old photo albums of the trips and her vast slide collection to cross check and to reminisce about the people met and the incredible sites throughout Cyprus. How lucky am I to have experienced the magic of Paphos with Pam, not just once in the trenches, but then again, years later, through this book.

Pam provides both a rounded and grounded view of the cultural, religious and economic context of the material record left by previous civilisations on the island of Aphrodite. I feel sure that you will enjoy Pam's stories of her visits to Cyprus and her extensive fieldwork as an 'amateur' archaeologist.

Dig in!
Julianne Deeb

*"Archaeology is not only the handmaid of History;
it is also the conservator of Art."*
Edward Bulmer Lytton

Chapter 1

A dream come true

"Hope springs eternal in the human breast"
Alexander Pope

I was nearly fifty years old and had taught ancient history for many years at a private school for girls in Brisbane. I wanted so much to work as an archaeologist - to get 'hands on' exposure to the origins of the history I taught.

The school bursar was often 'encouraging' me to take my long-service leave but I pointed out that I could not do anything because my mother was seriously ill and dependant on me. After she died, I had more time and began to plan. I applied for a scholarship from the University of Sydney to join a dig at Pella, in Jordan but was 'pipped at the post' by a geologist who had some very desirable skills.

One of my lecturers, Bruce Gollan – I was studying for a Master's Degree in Literary Studies – noticed my disappointment and said that he had a friend in Cyprus who was an archaeologist. A short time later, I was very excited to receive a letter from Dr Demetrios Michaelides inviting me to join the dig in Paphos, Cyprus.

I was thrilled and began planning immediately. My vet's daughters were able to live in my mother's home opposite my acreage, and care for my large menagerie of animals – a horse, donkeys, goats, pigs, dogs and cats. I took six months of long-service leave, saving three months for later, and was on my way. I flew to Larnaca, in Cyprus, via Athens. My adventure had begun.

My dream was about to come true and in preparation for its realisation, I went on a 'Grand Tour' of countries north and south of the Mediterranean Sea. An area which was significant in my knowledge of the ancient world – and a delightful and inspiring experience.

Chapter 2
The island of Aphrodite

"He who knows no history will always remain a child."
Marcus Tullius Cicero

I arrived in Paphos in February 1985, the flight from London landing late at night. I was finally there. I stayed at the Axiothea Hotel and transferred to the adjacent hotel apartments the next morning.

A few words to set the scene of the history, both ancient and modern, of the Republic of Cyprus.

Map of Mediterranean showing the geographical position of Cyprus

Map of Cyprus illustrating the major towns, including Paphos in the far south-west.

Cyprus is a relatively small island of 251 square km, lying south of Turkey (Anatolia) and on a clear day, that country can be seen from the north-east peninsula of Cyprus. Because it was situated close to so many ancient powers, it traded with or was invaded by Egypt, Persia, Anatolia, Lebanon, Greece and Rome. Therefore, it is rich in antiquities and attracts archaeologists from around the world. While I was in Paphos, teams were working there from Italy, Greece, Australia, England, the USA and Poland.

In 1878, Britain was granted control of Cyprus and ruled the island until it gained independence in 1960.

In 1974 Turkish forces invaded the island, claiming it as their own. There were many Turks living there already and relations between them and people of mainly Greek descent who had lived on the island for centuries had been largely amicable. The Turkish invasion was a tragedy. The invading forces captured most of the north of the island and the Cypriot Greek population fled south, becoming refugees.

A 'Green Line' was established, dividing the two areas and contact was either non-existent or belligerent.

Once as I was walking from Kato Paphos, the old Roman capital of the island to Ktima, the more recent upper town, I saw, seated on a bench halfway up the hill, an old lady weeping bitterly. I sat beside her to try to comfort her and found she was a refugee from the north who had lost everything.

Of recent years, it has become easier to cross the Green Line into the north – showing your passport if a visitor from outside Cyprus, or presenting documents if Cypriot. One of the areas seized included the airport of Nicosia, which is why flights use the airport at Larnaca.

I have visited the North several times, mainly to see the archeological sites, especially Salamis, the later Roman capital, which has been completely neglected by the Turkish authorities. The beautiful Gothic cathedral has been converted into a mosque. It was, however, a strange sensation to see the houses looking exactly the same as those over the border and fine British government buildings intact. Only the signs were different and of course the language was Turkish. The cars were very battered.

Cyprus was known in ancient times and still is today, as the island of Aphrodite, after the goddess of love and beauty, (called Venus by the Romans). According to mythology, she was born from seawater mixed with the sperm of the severed penis of the god Uranus. Aphrodite emerged from the foaming waves and came ashore in Cyprus.

The painting of this scene by the Renaissance artist, Botticelli, depicts the goddess in a large scallop shell; her golden hair partly obscuring her nakedness. Cypriots claim this happened at a very attractive spot called for some odd reason, *Petra tou Romiou* – or, stones of the Romans. It is a very beautiful rocky sea stack near Paphos.

Botticelli's Birth of Venus

Chapter 3

Mending my first pot

"Archaeology is like a jig-saw puzzle, except that you can't cheat and look at the box, and not all the pieces are there."

Stephen Dean

On my first morning I visited the Bank of Cyprus to ensure the arrangements I had made in Australia for drawing money were in place. I then found my way to the Museum, where I met Dr Michaelides (thereafter Demetri) and was immediately reassured. He told me of his plans for me - to work in the museum and, given the time of the year, some rescue archaeology!

The other members of staff were Petroula, who became a great friend, Takis the ephor (superintendent) of the museum and Androula, who kept the museum spick and span. The diggers were away on a rescue dig, where a tomb had been uncovered as a result of the telephone authorities mending a broken cable.

Pottery is one of the most valuable tools of the archaeologist and is usually abundant on ancient sites. I was set to work reassembling a pottery vessel stored in a metre-square, shallow, wooden tray which is the standard in Cyprus. Often when there were no trays available, we had to resort to cardboard boxes from the local supermarket! Right from the first pot when Petroula showed me the ropes, I really enjoyed this task.

Mending pottery under the eucalyptus tree

So many pottery sherds!

Of course, there were always broken sherds to wash, using a small, strong bristled brush. When we all sat in a circle with a full bucket of water in front of each of us, there was lots of cheerful conversation which reduced the tedium of the task. Once reconstructed, the vessel's shape can provide information about its place of origin, which in turn is useful for patterns of trade and for dating information.

Demetri explained that amphorae (two-handled pottery vessels) were used for storing wine, olive oil, garum and dry goods such as grain. Garum was fermented fish oil used for cooking which apparently had a repugnant smell.

Amphorae varied in shape according to its place of origin. Some amphorae had been found intact in a tomb and the handles were flat. The flat handles were stamped with the place of origin – the island of Rhodes – and indicated both the date and the ruler of one of Cyprus' trading partners. When the shape of the handles changed to curved, they could no longer be stamped and ceased to provide this useful information. Demetri wrote a very useful article on the significance of this discovery. Amphorae were sealed with clay and their shape also indicated their contents. For example, garum amphorae were smaller, with a restricted opening to allow the control of pouring the fish oil.

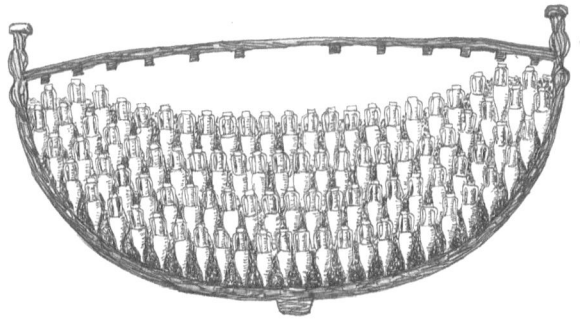

Amphora: Cross section of ship's hull showing the storage pattern of amphorae in transit

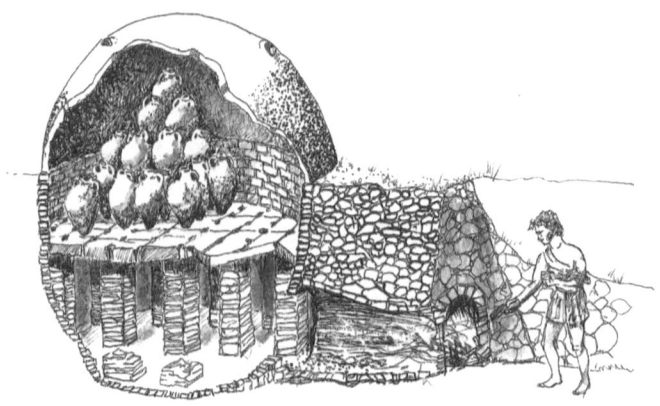

Amphora: Kiln design and stacking arrangement
for making amphorae

My first task was to mend a pot, the remains of which, from the number of sherds indicated it was probably a cooking pot. Their shape was less likely to change because once a convenient shape was established, there was no need to alter it. My pot had obviously been left on the stove too long because it was black on the inside and a paler grey outside. When I discovered two matching pieces of a pot, I was shown how to use two pencil-lines across the join. I was very pleased with myself when I found a number of matching pieces. Why, one might ask, did cooking pots need to be reconstructed, since they usually maintained their shape? The reason is that different shapes may have developed for different uses and could be a clue to diet. The ancient Cypriot diet appears to have been a healthy one!

The pieces were stuck together with glue – often with many gaps – working from the base to the rim. Demetri admitted that one of his favourite jobs was mending pottery and it became mine too.

Where's My Bucket and Spade?

Three amphorae in stands

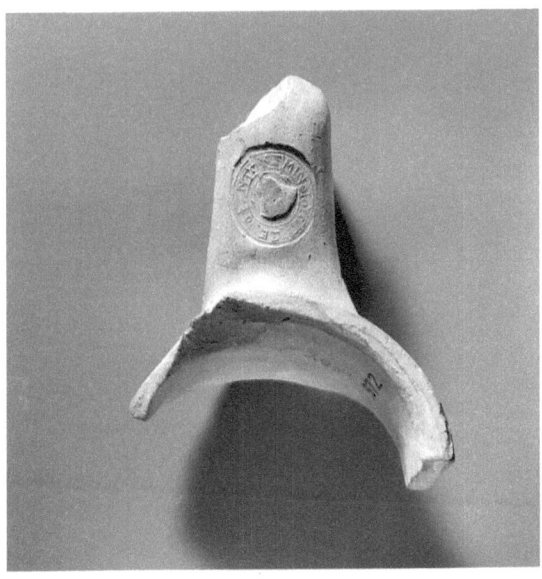

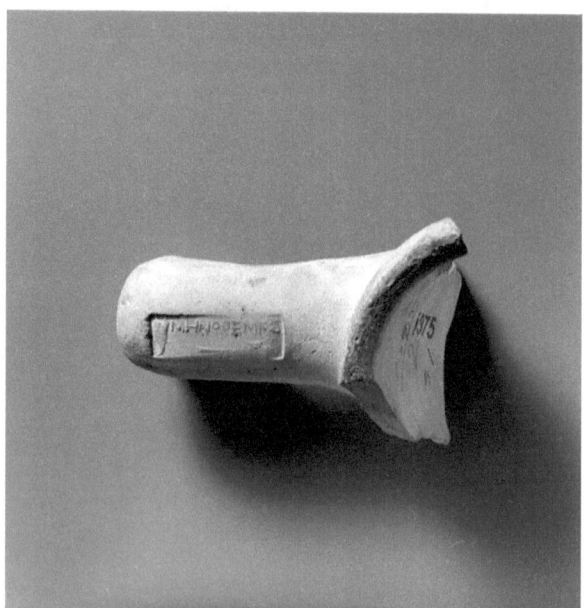

Stamped handles of amphorae

Chapter 4

A pleasant routine

"The trivial round, the common task will furnish all we need to ask."

John Keble

After I had been mending and washing pots in the museum, I developed a routine. I shopped and visited the bank on Saturday mornings and in the afternoons spent happy times with the friends I had made – Petroula who often took me to her home for lunch; Anne and her husband John who were English but retired to Cyprus because he had been stationed there with the British in World War II; and Helen, a Scottish lady from Oban who had an apartment in Kato Paphos and spent most of the spring and early summer in Paphos. On one notable occasion lunching with Helen, she suggested I test her Vespa, a 'gentle' motor-cycle which would allow me to travel further afield. The experiment was a dismal failure. I had never learned to ride a bicycle and really preferred to ride a horse because it had something on each corner. Luckily, the Vespa and I were not harmed, but my main mode of travel remained by foot.

When I was not lunching with Anne and John at their beautiful home in the hills or with Helen, a local Cypriot would scoop me up for a meal. The Cypriots are extraordinarily hospitable. I was invited to weddings and other family celebrations. I also spent many happy meals with Demetri, his wife Sarah and their three boys. Later, a daughter Pamela, was added to the family.

After several weeks in Cyprus, I added assisting Demetri who had helped me so much, to my Saturday routine. I wrote to the librarian at my school, Somerville House, to ask him to provide the Dewey classifications for the relevant subjects and after I received his reply, catalogued the museum library, providing a book for people to record their borrowings. Previously, the library had been a shambles.

I was a frequent visitor to the town library. It had an excellent range of English books which I devoured quickly and soon returned for more, always surprising the librarian at how quickly I finished them. Demetri often provided me with weekend reading on subjects such as recognising different animal bones.

It was a busy life and I enjoyed it. When Demetri announced I was to take part in a rescue dig in the main street of Ktima (Neo Paphos) I was over the moon.

Chapter 5

Ancient discoveries

"Archaeology is the peeping Tom of the sciences. It is the sandbox of men who care not where they are going; they merely want to know where everyone else has been."

James Bishop

I was full of anticipation as I walked with Demetri to the site in one of the main streets of Ktima (Neo Paphos). The diggers, including Neoptolemos, a local who regularly worked with Demetri, had been exploring a tomb discovered earlier. It had yielded nothing. 'My tomb', however, was more promising.

A telephone company's cable had been severed and the attempts to clear it had revealed the tombs. It was a 'rescue' of the Roman era tombs we were performing. The bulldozer being used for the operation was very large, and as it was working so near to our tomb, we had to emerge hurriedly whenever it was overhead, lest it descend upon us. This was an unusual hazard on my first dig.

I met the two diggers, one of whom was named Chrysanthos, and they were a delight. They were excavating diggers, not archaeologists. Both men were short – a definite advantage for crawling into small spaces and neither spoke any English but I could interpret their gestures very easily. One of the men prided himself on his extraordinarily acute vision. On one dig, Demetri told me, he had found a needle, not in a haystack, but on a dirt floor. I was quite triumphant once while on a sieving task to find a small sherd he had missed. He was mortified.

Diggers on site- Kyriakou and Chrysanthos

When excavating, I soon learned that I could not kneel, which is the normal position archaeologists adopted. I sat and excavated to my side. Some people chose to stand and bend over but, being tall, that made me dizzy. My tools were a small brush and a scraper for the fine work, and as I set

My sitting down style of digging

to work I was pleased to find the tomb largely undisturbed. There were a few broken objects to clean, but the skeletons were beyond my expertise at that time. There were a number of rich items, suggesting at least one female occupant, was a glass spindle whorl, the type used in the spinning process, though glass would have been impractical for use. An ivory trinket box lid also suggests a female occupant and probably the ivory would have been sourced from Africa – either directly or through an intermediate source. A decorated oyster shell from the Persian Gulf demonstrates the extent of Cyprus' foreign trade in luxury goods.

I also found a special rare violet glass perfume bottle, the origin of which was unknown – perhaps from the East or perhaps local. There were some gold leaf pieces, broken pots and scattered leg, foot and toe bones. The three skeletons were arranged, two below and one on top – pushed to the side though still articulated, one with 'ooze' coming from its mouth, indicating it was moved while still not fully decomposed.

Later, I would be allowed to clean skeletons, but it was such a specialised skill, that I had to leave finishing it to the experts so that the forensic team could uncover its secrets. The study of skeletons in Paphos yielded information about leukemia (Mediterranean Thalassemia). Evidence of trepanation (a process by which pressure was alleviated by drilling a hole in the skull following a head injury or sometimes to release evil spirits from the mentally ill) was also found. Part of the patient's skull was removed by a boring process – without pain relief – but it did work on occasions and had been practised in Egypt for centuries.

At 3.30pm we left the dig – for me a very enjoyable day in which I learned a great deal. At 7.00 the next morning we returned, eager for the next challenge and were joined by my Scottish friend, Helen.

The earth-moving team had removed the heavy equipment, so that made our job a little easier. Neoptolemos was a very good teacher – even-tempered, patient and was able to clearly explain what he wanted. I cleaned the soil from around the loose bones, which seemed to be in mixed order. We found four skulls and bones, not well preserved – piled 'higgledy-piggledy' on the ground and Helen found an attractive glass bottle. The men working in the other chamber found a needle, a few pieces of gold and not much else. I learned so much but it was rather tiring, as I was bent double all the time.

Chapter 6

My life in ruins

"My Life in Ruins"
                    Adam Ford

Sunday was my day for exploring archaeological sites, which I could visit either by walking or bus – the only public transport available, or by service taxi, a type of shared taxi service used throughout the middle east and Greece. I ventured first to Kato Paphos, walking from the apartment, down the hill at a brisk pace as it was early March and still quite cold. The many small boats were drawn up on the pebbly beach as the sea was winter-rough, the crashing waves adding to the bleakness of the day.

The fort would have been interesting to explore but was not open to the public. It resembled a very similar building in Crete. I investigated the souvenir shops – definitely not ruins but doing good trade for the tourists. A well-known local pelican, which had become something of a symbol of Kato Paphos, was strutting confidently along the sea wall as I passed. Having enjoyed a tasty Cypriot take-away, I went in search of the 'ruins' that I had been told were nearby.

The backway to return to the apartments seemed the most likely prospect to locate the sites and sure enough, there it was – the church called Ayia Kyriaki, sitting on the ruins of an early Christian basilica known as the Chrysopolitissa, with the pillar of St Paul beside it. One of the reasons that there were so many churches in the area was the belief that

Paul had been tied to the pillar and flayed. In fact, the pillar is later than the First Century A.D. so the story was apocryphal. To gain access, I had to climb through a hole in the wire fence beside the church. Stepping inside, I mused over its origins and subsequently made some discoveries.

In the ruins of the Chrysopolitissa, there were fine mosaics but they were from the later basilica which is built on the ruins. Geometrical in style, the mosaics also depicted animals and Biblical themes. The mosaics were very attractive, with no intrusive architectural features. The columns were predominantly bluish-grey, yellow and green – several of them at a lower level than the present church. Many of them are spoils from the nearby Roman theatre, and are in secondary use. Were they from the sixth century or earlier I wondered? Four great granite columns are associated with the early basilica, while the so-called St Paul's pillar is a column of grey-blue Proconnesian marble, erected several centuries after the Saint's visit. The columns seemed to be of the Hadrianic period and were Corinthian, tipped with acanthus leaves. A large geometric floor area similar to the Pantheon rested on a higher level than the mosaics (2nd Century A.D.).

The wall decoration and size of the columns could suggest a very large house or public building. If it were a public building, why was it *outside* the city walls? The columns appeared to be from the later Christian period.

A little further away I came across what looked to be the remains of a Gothic church, with some characteristic pillars sawn off, built on the ruins of the early Christian basilica. This was Ayios Georghios tes Peyias, north-west of Paphos. The modern church of St George is a solid, panelled, vaulted building, not particularly attractive but interesting due to its grandeur.

My first attempts at interpreting archaeological ruins were substantially supported by Demetri – thank goodness!

In a later discussion, Demetri added some information about Ayios Georghios (St George) which he interpreted as Justinian (5th Century A.D.).

Its columns were of Proconnesian marble from the Sea of Marmara near Istanbul, probably imported complete from Constantinople, with Byzantine capitals of the style similar to other Justinian churches – for example St John's Church at Ephesus. The mosaics near the apse displayed sea creatures and an inscription on the pulpit screen showed it was associated with sailors using the nearby harbour. Near the sunken baptistry, similar to St John's at Ephesus, were badly deteriorated mosaics of a bull, lion, bear and another animal, which was not necessarily associated with the Four Apostles. Other animals such as a donkey were also depicted in the basilica. There is evidence that a small basilica was built into the transept of the Justinian structure.

What an exciting introduction to my life in ruins!

Chapter 7

Reading the ruins

"While in the progress of their long decay, thrones sink to dust and nations pass away."
          Earl of Carlisle, 'On the Ruins of Paestum'

When I was teaching, my students often asked me how buildings or even whole cities disappeared under the soil. One weekend, I accompanied Sarah, Demetri and the boys on a brief holiday in the Troodos Mountains. The boys wanted me to take them to the abandoned hotel nearby. Named the Berengaria after the wife of Richard I of England, it had been a luxury holiday venue from earlier in the Twentieth Century, and had later housed Greek Cypriot refugees from the 1974 invasion. The boys were looking for objects the refugees had left behind and wanted to explore upstairs but I vetoed that because the stairs looked unsafe.

Meanwhile, I was intrigued by the signs of decay already visible, providing a perfect example of how sites are covered after only twenty years – since the refugees had been re-homed.

The rotting timber roof struts had allowed water in to hasten the decay. All the windows had been broken, presumably by vandals, so dust and leaves were blown in. The dirt and dust may have carried seeds which would have germinated, adding to the destruction, though this had not occurred when I visited. No doubt, scavengers would have taken building material as well, leading to more rapid decay. It would be interesting to see it now.

Of course, some cities or even civilisations are destroyed by natural disasters or even local geographical phenomena. Pompeii, Herculaneum and other towns in the area of Mount Vesuvius when it erupted in 79 A.D., were completely covered either by pumice or lava. It is always surprising to me that, although there were many survivors, (and even Pliny the Younger's written account of his uncle's death), there is no evidence of survivors returning to reclaim property or bodies of family members. On the other hand, the trauma that the survivors experienced must have been too great. It was not until the eighteenth century that work began on excavating these.

The wonderful Roman-Syrian city of Palmyra was abandoned when the ruling family's power declined and Roman commercial activity diminished. It was gradually covered by sand blown from the surrounding desert. The beautiful, richly-decorated Roman architecture, the Temple of Hadrian and the arch at the crossroads, as well

The theatre at Palmyra, Syria

as the theatre, were well preserved by the all-enveloping sand. Sadly, these wonderfully innovative structures were subsequently completely destroyed by militant Muslim groups. I had met the ephor of the museum in Palmyra and he was a delightful man, who was tragically killed when, during the attack he refused to divulge where he had hidden precious museum items. So Palmyra has been lost again, never to be recovered.

Another way in which sites are covered, is by what archaeologists call 'hill wash'. When a hillside is bare of enough vegetation to hold the soil in place, that soil will be washed down the hill, especially in heavy rain. Any settlements at the foot, unable to cope with the amount of soil accumulated there, will be abandoned and in time, will be lost. Changes in water levels are yet another factor. Off the coast of Alexandria in northern Egypt, a French team of underwater archaeologists found ruins of the Ptolemaic period, about 300 BC to 100 AD. They had hoped to find the tomb of Cleopatra but there has been no success as yet.

Aerial photography has been used widely in countries which have extensive agricultural activity and more recent ruins. England is a good case in point where aerial photography has exposed medieval three field systems. Ground-penetrating radar is also a useful modern tool; seen extensively on the TV series 'Time Team'.

Let's not forget the constantly alert brain and gimlet eyes of the trained archaeologist! I remember, walking in the car park of the dig site, when Demetri pointed out a row of stones, protruding slightly above the ground. He asked what I thought they signified. Since I had no idea, he explained they were the top of a wall; and would be excavated at a later date. So functioned the mind of a trained archaeologist.

Chapter 8

Exploring Paphos and Kourion

"There is a beauty in ruins to those who see."
                                    Emmanuel Rajkumar

On another Sunday exploration of the ruins surrounding Paphos I visited the so-called 'Tombs of the Kings' as it was within walking distance of my apartment. The whole area was blooming with spring flowers – cyclamen, daisies and poppies. The tombs dating from the Hellenistic period, about 300 B.C., have a few Roman burials. Many tombs are excavated from the rock with loculi and niches in the walls. There are, however, four or five tombs with atria and the burial places opening from them. The atria are entered by

The tombs of the kings site

way of a dromos with a varying number of steps and often a panel-vaulted ceiling. Sometimes stucco survives in the atria. They have either square or round columns, some with Doric capitals and triglyphs and metopes on the entablature.

There is a well found under the colonnade, probably used for ritual purposes. The burial chambers open off the atria with varying numbers of loculi and niches with sometimes a cippus, a low pedestal marking a grave.

In one or two places, the remains of wall paintings or frescoes are visible on the plaster work. Only one tomb differs markedly from the usual pattern. It has a large burial area in the centre of a courtyard with decorative plasterwork above the doorways of the various chambers, as well as niches and loculi in the wall of the courtyard with two entrances to the dromoi. Many of the tombs were re-used and slightly damaged or enlarged in Roman times. The style of the tombs seems to have been modelled on Hellenistic houses from Asia Minor.

After enjoying the satisfying and enlightening experience of exploring the tombs, I sat under a shady tree near the tombs with a book. Imagine my surprise when 'Scotland the Brave' sounded loudly from the nearby rise! It emanated from a Scotsman in a kilt. While I love the sound of bagpipes, I was certainly struck by the incongruity of the 300 B.C. tombs and a kilt-clad Scotsman playing the bagpipes in the 20th century!

I did not need to go exploring the Byzantine fortress known as Saranda Kolones, on a Sunday as it was next door to our dig at Kato Paphos. It is called the 'fortress of the forty columns' and stands in a commanding position. Some of the grey granite columns lie around the perimeter as well as a few capitals and decorations of Byzantine type. An American team had been excavating there for several years and Demetri knew them well. Relations with our team and theirs were very friendly and how grateful I was to one of the team, Victoria, who comforted me after I had received the news that my horse, Patch, had died of colic.

Saranda Kolones site

There was one site which we were not invited to visit – the so-called 'Garrison Camp', though in fact it was later discovered to be an ancient ritual area. We were all amused, when the Italian team arrived to see that their first priority was securing shade cloth, deck chairs and pot plants. All seemed to be frequently in use during the day.

A few weeks later I was delighted by an invitation by Sarah and Demetri to visit Kourion (Curium according to Roman nomenclature). It is an evocative site on the coast – east of Paphos and stands on a hill, which provides natural protection. On a rise above the remains of the town stands the Temple of Apollo Hylates. The columns are Nabatean in form and seem to date from the second rebuilding (circa 2nd Century A.D.). The temple is not typically Greek. It has been restored at only one end probably because the rest of the materials were no longer there. It stands on a podium with twelve steps leading to the entrance. There is a colonnade only at the front and inside there is a pronaos and naos where the statue of the deity would have stood, making it very Roman in appearance.

After looking with appreciation at the Temple of Apollo Hylates, we walked to the townsite. As we moved through the various areas, I stored up questions in my mind to assess whether my ability to read a site had improved. Certain features which indicated a water supply were evident – baths, a nymphaeum and so on. Demetri explained that were was an aqueduct supplying water to the nymphaeum and it was one of the first to be studied in Cyprus. A number of cisterns also exist which may either pre- or post-date the aqueduct. The nymphaeum is a shrine to the nymphs of the woodland. Demetri is inclined to think that the cisterns were added when the aqueduct no longer functioned well or its source dried up and the cisterns took over the water supply, with drains providing the input. Run-off from the roofs of the houses and other buildings would have provided the water for the cisterns. My belief is that a good water supply and effective drains are the basis of civilisation!

An element of the nymphaeum is an area for sacred physical activity – the dressing rooms, the palaestra or exercise area, priest's house and stadium. Also the baths, that Roman feature, are to be found in all urban areas and in the wealthier private houses. There were three room, a hot room or caldarium, warm room or tepidarium and the cold room or the frigidarium – which sounds rather daunting! It was often a plunge bath. The hypocaust, which heats the water for the hot and warm rooms, as the name suggests was usually below the floor on either round or square tile columns – square being the most common. Sometimes, the hypocaust was above ground adjoining the building and the hot air travelled to the rooms by pipes.

The Agora (or Forum in the Roman period) is well-preserved and a vivid evocation of Greek and Roman public life. The Stoa was a public building which provided a place for discussions and for philosophers to argue their views and attract a following. The debates must have been lively in both Athens and in Kourion! Lying in the Stoa in Kourion is a twisted column with a Corinthian capital. According to Demetri, it probably dates to the Hadrianic period, the early Second Century A.D. I was pleased to hear that as part of the refurbishment of the site, it is now standing upright.

Our next port of call was the Theatre. It is below the top of the hill on which the city is situated – a distance above the sea. It has a very large semi-circular Orchestra with a curving stage. Demetri said that it doubled as a site for gladiatorial games and wild beast shows as well. The former is supported by mosaics from the House of the Gladiators, dating from the Roman period. The two contestants are depicted with blunted swords, while a referee stands watching to ensure fair play. Scholars are divided whether this depicts a practice session, the cut-off swords designed to prevent injury, or a less violent form of the sport. As far as I know, there is no definitive evidence for wild beast shows.

There was one more exciting area to visit before we left the site. The archaeologist David Soren had excavated a large, private house. The columns supporting the colonnade were of high quality but seemed to have fallen on hard times, because there was archaeological evidence the area had become a farm. There, in a collapsed shed, he found the bodies of a young girl and a donkey under a collapsed beam from the roof. They were victims of the 4th century earthquake which also had dire effects in Paphos. I felt compassion for the girl and her donkey. They are displayed in the Episkopi Museum in a nearby town, with all the finds from Kourion (Curium).

We made our way back to Paphos and I felt so privileged to have explored Kourion with Demetri, such a knowledgeable guide and my thanks to Sarah our chauffeur. I felt more confident that I was managing to interpret sites more correctly – a necessity for a working archaeologist.

The site at Kourion and the theatre

Chapter 9

Cypriot hospitality over the Troodos Mountains

"The word 'hospitality' in the New Testament comes from two Greek words. The first word means 'love' and the second word means 'strangers'. It's a word that means 'love of strangers."

Nancy Leigh DeMoss

I had only about a month left of my long service leave. The time had flown, it was now summer in Cyprus – up to 40 degrees in Paphos. Because the town was beside the sea it was a humid heat and rather debilitating. The work went on! There were still pots to be washed and mended, rescue sites to be dug and, since the official digging season had begun, the continuing work on the House of Orpheus in Kato Paphos, to be addressed. Of this, more later.

I accompanied Sarah and Demetri to Nicosia, the capital of Cyprus to stay with Demetri's parents. I enjoyed the visit very much. His mother was so welcoming and an entertaining conversationalist. His father I found rather intimidating. He was a very highly regarded paediatrician He appeared to speak no English. Later, however, when I got to know him better, I found he spoke good English and I enjoyed our conversations. Sarah and Demetri had family commitments and I spent a fruitful time exploring the National Archaeological Museum and getting to know the history of Cyprus by way of its artefacts.

Nicosia was also very hot, but a dry heat so much easier to tolerate. One amusing incident occurred at lunch on the day we left. Demetri's father offered me a glass of ouzo. Courtesy demanded that I accept, though I was completely unused to alcohol. I gather I talked all the way back to Paphos but made little sense! It took me a while to live that down and ouzo was off the menu in future!

On another trip, Sarah and Demetri took me to Larnaca on the west coast. This was another memorable occasion, expanding my knowledge in my quest to interpret ruins. Larnaca is a busy commercial hub, the airport of Cyprus on its outskirts. Often that is all that visitors see of this interesting city. We visited the House of Pierides, a fine two-storied Cyprus stone building, restored to its glorious past. It has pillared verandas in the front, allowing light and cool breezes to enter the building. It reminded me, to some extent, of the homes of early settlers in Australia, though they were rarely of stone, nor two-storied. The Pierides House was one of the grandest houses surviving but there were many such structures, though less grand, scattered through this charming town.

The Pierides Museum features a fine collection of Cypriot antiquities, including Bronze Age Cypriot bronzes and Cypriot silk. The island was noted for its silk production. I remember visiting the folk museum in Paphos dedicated to that most industrious creature, the silkworm. The sound of their chewing was almost deafening! Paper bags, each one containing a worm, were attached to the wall as they devoured inordinate numbers of mulberry leaves. I was transported back to my childhood but my silkworms were housed in a box and produced only enough to make a bookmark.

We could not linger long in the Pierides Museum, since the site of Kiti beckoned. Kiti is fascinating to an amateur archaeologist. On the site is a beautiful surviving church of the pre-iconoclastic movement of the Sixth Century A.D. Larnaca was an important Arab enclave and that may have helped protect the church from the predations of the iconoclasts.

As part of the site, we visited the salt lake on the bank on which is a shrine to a member of Mahommet the Prophet's family. Although the flamingos were only just making an appearance, their bright pink plumage made my heart sing!

Lest the reader be under the illusion that my life consisted entirely of travelling to sites, I assure you that digging was in progress! There was a mound, near the House of Orpheus, our permanent site which some older inhabitants told me had been a gun emplacement during 'the troubles'. Demetri decided to do a rescue dig and removing the top soil revealed mosaics! The site was named the Baths of Triton. The central figure of Triton was in coloured stone tesserae while at each entrance was a panther, the animal associated with Dionysus.

I was very aware that my time in Cyprus was drawing to a close and was determined to make the most of my opportunities to learn. As well as digging in the House of Orpheus, I saw more of the local sites with Demetri as guide. There was a new mosaic, recently uncovered, but recovered to protect it. Demetri cleared part of it and put water on it to show me how water brought the colours to life. This is not a practice normally undertaken because of possible damage to mosaics but it was only for a moment. We also visited a tomb which Demetri had excavated in 1983. Due to the popularity of Paphos as a growing tourist resort, the urgent excavation of tombs was essential. I was shown one of these tombs which was situated on land not far from the new mosaic. The grave goods of course had been disturbed and removed. Nearby, on the beach front, black-faced sheep were guarded by a vigilant shepherd – a charming rural scene!

There are several highlights of my first visit to Cyprus. On one occasion on the return visit from Nicosia, Sarah, an extraordinarily competent driver, drove Demetri, the boys and me via the Troodos Mountains to Paphos. It had been particularly cold resulting in a very heavy snowfall. I was in awe of Sarah's skill in navigating the treacherous conditions. It was very beautiful and the boys (and I) had a wonderful time playing in the snow. I had never seen so much snow!

Another precious memory is being taken to the church in Asinou where Sarah and Demetri and Sarah were married. It is in an isolated position in the mountains and dates to the 12th Century A.D. I remember collecting the key from the nearest town, because the church is quite isolated. It commonly experiences snowfalls so has a steeply pointed roof, as do other churches in the area. When we entered the church, I was stunned by the wonderful wall paintings. On one side of the entrance were depictions of the joys awaiting the righteous and on the other, the highly inventive punishments awaiting the doomed. Around the walls were small panels depicting individual 'crimes', for example stealing fruit from a neighbour's tree.

In the same area, also subject to snowfalls, is St Nicholas of the Roof (Agios Nicolaus tis Stegis) with a very steep roof and wooden verandas as protection for the church-goers. It dates to the 11th Century and the stunning frescoes are much more Byzantine and formalised in their presentation.

Another memorable occasion was Greek Easter. My Scottish friend Helen and I were hiking in the hills north of Cyprus and found many people enjoying picnics. It was 'Clean Monday', the beginning of Lent, when only vegetables are eaten. Weeks later, Easter was commemorated. On Thursday night each parish provided two members to carry the Epitafios through the streets of the town. The dead body of Christ was depicted in a painting and the parishes were rather proud and competitive in their depictions. On Saturday, the Holy

Where's My Bucket and Spade?

The Church of Panagia of Asinou

Detail of one of the many frescoes

Flame was brought from Jerusalem. Today it comes by air, in the past by sea. It must not be extinguished.

Then we attended Midnight Service. At Greek Orthodox Easter, the priest proclaims that "Christ is risen" though it is not yet known to his followers. Then each Epitafios is covered with offerings of flowers. 'EPITAFIOS' means 'on the tomb'. The members of the congregation each light a candle from the Holy Flame and walk around the church several times. All try to ensure their flames reach home still alight.

It was very moving but because it was very hot and there were no seats, I disgraced myself by fainting! The congregation walked with lighted candles around the exterior of the church and strove to reach the place to celebrate Christ's resurrection with the candles still alight. The fast was broken with a celebratory meal.

Easter was a very moving experience but it was not quite over. On Easter Monday, the villagers celebrated with games. Helen took me to a little village where the young men were enthusiastically engaged in races and other athletic feats. I was amused to see the very elderly priest wandering vaguely onto the racing track. It was like an incident from the bull-running in Spain. At the last minute, before the runners knocked him over, an onlooker rushed out and swept him out of danger.

What an extraordinary and moving Easter it had been.

Chapter 10

The Customs House and first farewell

"Monuments and archaeological pieces serve as testimonies of man's greatness and establish a dialogue between civilisations showing the extent to which human beings are linked."

Vincente Fox

Wednesday 23rd June was the most exciting day for me – the beginning of a rescue dig! I had been busy excavating the House of Orpheus and finding interesting objects in corners and at the base of walls.

Late in the afternoon, Demetri had a message that some worked stones had been found when the machinery was being used to excavate the site for new public toilets down by the harbour.

Demetri commented that we would investigate the following day though there was probably little to find. All work on the House of Orpheus site ceased. The next morning the team gathered – Petroula, the three diggers and I.

Preliminary work began. The soil was rather ashy and easy to excavate. The site was outside the city walls. On one side was the very solid Customs House, built by the British administration and on the other side, a large Aquarium building, so the site was quite restricted in area.

At the end of the day, a skeleton was uncovered, lying in the middle of the site. As is so common, something of importance is often found just when excavations are finishing for the day. I commented that I would photograph the find in case local dogs disturbed it!

Although I was to leave Cyprus in just over a week, I worked on the 'Public Toilet Dig' (subsequently called the Customs House Dig, as a more salubrious title), with increasing enthusiasm. I was given the task of cleaning the original skeleton, using a small brush. That was exciting! The workmen excavated several skulls, the bodies of which were under the two neighbouring buildings.

Up the slope, Demetri was uncovering more complete skeletons. Each had the arms clasped on the chest indicating Christian burials.

Because I have small hands, Demetri asked me to insert my hand into a deep cavity, under the large stone, at the lower end of the trench. I did so rather tentatively. "Is there some nasty sea creature which will nip me?" I wondered. Then the vision of cockroaches flashed into my mind; these were my *bêtes noires*. I was terrified of the big black ones with a circle of white around their heads! All was well – there were only more stones…

The House of Orpheus was excavated using square trenches with baulks, as baulks in between provided convenient access for wheelbarrows to collect the excavated soil and remove it to the spoil-heap away from the excavation. Our dig at the Custom's House was 'open area' because of the nature of the site. American archaeologists tend to use 'open area' for their sites. I have excavated many burials and while I enjoy the challenge, I always treat the bodies with respect. I believe revealing them and finding something of their lives, gives them a new importance and significance.

At first, it seemed the bodies were those of monks from the nearby monastery. They were all male with only one younger boy. It transpired, however, that the burials dated to the 6th or 7th Centuries A.D., before the monastery was built. The forensic archaeologists were able to date the bones and it was decided that they had either died of an outbreak of disease or since there were no women or children, that they were Cypriot warriors killed in fighting against the Arab invaders.

Meanwhile I was preparing to leave Cyprus while the team was still working. On 30th June, the day before I was to leave Paphos, the staff had a farewell party, with all sorts of delicious Cypriot finger food. I was moved, too, by their gifts to me. I was very reluctant to leave, but I had some more long-service leave and would return to Cyprus. My almost six months there had changed my life. After the sad years of Mother's illness and death, Cyprus was the fulfillment of my dream; I had my new 'family', Sarah, Demetri and the boys, and generous friends.

On leaving Cyprus I flew to Heraklion, Crete. It was a wonderful site and visitors were still able to enter the various rooms of the Palace of Knossos, a privilege now denied because the frescoes were being damaged by visitors 'breathing!' I loved investigating the intricate and highly efficient drainage system. My favourite room was the Queen's Megaron with the lovely Dolphin Frescoes. I was irritated by a group of German tourists who noisily chattered during the guide's explanation. She finally cried out in furious voice, "Will you shut up!" (They certainly did not appreciate how privileged they were.)

The importance of the sensitive display of an excavated site really came home to me here.

After a few days in Crete, I returned to Brisbane and began teaching one day later!

Chapter 11

The lifting of the Mosaic of Orpheus

*"Or bid the soul of Orpheus sing
such notes as, warbled to the string,
drew iron tears down Pluto's cheek"*
                    John Milton

On Monday 11th June 1989, I arrived in Larnaca for my much anticipated second visit to Cyprus and to spend three months of my long service leave there. Since the flight arrived too late to travel to Paphos then, I stayed in Larnaca and travelled to Paphos in the morning. It was a very nostalgic journey, which brought back happy memories of my previous visit. There was the sight of the British Army Camp and the soldiers jogging in the forty-degree heat. 'Mad dogs and Englishmen?' Then there was the stunning glimpse of the birthplace of Aphrodite, and many other memories.

I made my way to the museum where I was greeted warmly by the staff. There was an air of excitement mixed with some anxiety because the following day the mosaic of Orpheus at Paphos was to be returned to its original position within the House of Orpheus after being taken away to be stabilised and the ground prepared to receive it. This was acknowledged to be an innovative and potentially dangerous procedure for the mosaic. The site where the House of Orpheus stood was a key area of focus for the department of antiquities at that time and it was UNESCO world heritage listed in 1980. It formed part of a large archaeological site where other houses had been excavated, each named after the mosaic located within, including the House of Dionysus and the House of Theseus.

I had not seen the removal of the large Orpheus mosaic which had taken place some 8 months before I arrived. The mosaic was in danger of cracking because the base soil was subsiding. A large wooden roller was used and the mosaic was lifted by crane to a nearby cement base where the restoration team from the Getty Institute worked on it for some time. It was certainly a complex task involving a large team of specialists who patiently conserved the tesserae and returned the glorious mosaic to its beauty.

While the mosaic (which took up nearly the whole room and measured 2.8m x 3.4m) was being conserved, the team continued excavating the site, which was a large house on a beautiful spot near the coast. Aristodemos, a volunteer and a friend of Demetri's was excavating a cesspit discovered nearby – not a salubrious job but necessary! Aristodemos and I were to have many adventures over the years. Also, a former student of mine, Julianne Deeb, who happened to be involved in the dig and her friend from Brisbane, Andrea had been given the task to excavate down to bedrock, underneath where the mosaic had been and to where it would return. This was seen as a rare chance to see what was under the mosaic and it was interesting to hear that there was more than a metre of excavation, representing successive time periods prior to the Roman house, which was dated to late second, early third century AD.

This is where I entered the drama. Two days after I arrived, the mosaic was to be repositioned back into its original place in the room where it had been. We all knew how fraught with danger this day was and a crowd of supporters gathered.

Pamela Davenport

Aristodemos digging in the cesspit

Demetri at the House of Orpheus

We arrived at the site to see the Getty team already at work. They were a polyglot group which sometimes caused amusing or irritating situations. The leader was Werner Schmidt, a Czech who spoke barely any English but fluent Italian. Paolo Pastorello, an Italian with little English, Clara Dean, an American who spoke only English, and Demetri overseeing the whole procedure. Fortunately, he spoke English, Greek and Italian fluently. His job was to interpret and to keep the expats calm and focused. The group of bystanders – including Sarah and the boys, Aristodemos, Julianne and Andrea, the American team working on nearby Saranda Kolones, our neighbours 'and Uncle Tom Cobbly and all' stood on a slight rise overlooking the position where the mosaic was to be replaced. The Cypriot diggers tried to look busy with their usual excavation task but I have no doubt they had glimpses of the activities around the mosaic.

The audience watching the mosaic being moved

Mosaic on the wooden roller and the big crane

The crane arrived and we all watched anxiously as it picked up the mosaic. One could almost hear the indrawn breaths from the onlookers when it became clear that the arm of the crane was too short to move the mosaic into position. The mosaic had to be rested against a roller while the crane repositioned. We were all so anxious lest the mosaic fall and shatter as it was picked up again. But luckily all was well and the mosaic was safely restored in place.

History had been made! It was the first time such a delicate operation (crane and large wooden roller) with a mosaic had been attempted and it was successful! We couldn't wait to see the mosaic once it was cleaned and the conservators checked everything was in order.

The following day the television cameramen arrived to celebrate on film the unveiling of the mosaic. This was another very exciting event! Everyone held their breath as

Mosaic being carefully lifted in the air

Mosaic being lifted back to its original location, with a new concrete base

Buongiorno Orfeo! The mosaic revealed, the water shows the brilliant colours

TV crew filming the reveal of the restored mosaic

the beauty of the mosaic was revealed with a bucket of water thrown over it! One of the Italian team leaders exclaimed enthusiastically, *"Buongiorno Orfeo!"* Relieved applause followed, it really was a joy to behold. The mosaic looked so beautiful with a cream background and the figures of Orpheus and the animals in shades of brown floating on the background. The simple border displayed a geometric design.

The detail of Orpheus' clothing was distinct and together with the lyre was very well preserved.

Detail of Orpheus from the mosaic

Demetri was now to cover the mosaic with a protective canopy so it could be displayed for the public. He found an Australian company who provided the necessary protection. This lasted for many years until a severe storm destroyed it. For protection, the mosaic was covered with a tarpaulin and small stones – so it sadly remains today. After the mosaic drama we continued the excavation of the site of the House of Orpheus. Julianne found a well-preserved Roman coin in the topsoil close to the remains of the wall of a room. I found a piece of folded lead. I was excited because I thought it was a 'curse' tablet. This was an object which the Greeks and Romans believed would bring dire consequences to a person whose name was scratched on a piece of lead together with a curse. I soon realised it was not such an object because they were placed in tombs normally.

Julianne and I discovered a block of worked stone with a plaster covering, partly decorated with fresco. I was intrigued to see one of the workmen prepared it for removal. It was covered with sheets of tissue paper, then layers of gauze. The following day, the plaster with the fresco was removed from the block of stone. It was in the Fourth Style with a white background and swirls in red and green. We realised that the most productive area for small finds was close to walls and corners of rooms. I found amongst the uncompacted soil in a corner, some rather 'nice' sherds, a lamp in a characteristic grey-colour and the top of a black-glazed Hellenistic lamp with a larger opening than usual.

The workmen were excavating the baths of the house of Orpheus which had the usual rooms but very interesting features. First, they had entrances to both the adjoining street and to the house, suggesting that they were used by the local people as well as by the household. The second unusual feature was the round tiles used in the hypocaust – usually such tiles were square.

I had been in Cyprus almost a week and my luggage was still in Budapest! This was a nightmare not infrequently suffered by international travellers. Sarah lent me some night clothes and a few 'digging clothes'. When the airport at Larnaca finally delivered the errant suitcase, quite a number of items were missing. Most of the clothing items had been rejected by the thieves – presumably not to their sartorial taste – but many of my gifts to the team had gone. As well as my swimsuit, which was replaced by one which did not fit! At least I had 'digging' wardrobe.

Chapter 12

Uncovering unguentaria and skeletons

"Skeletons are like hidden treasures, waiting to be uncovered."

Source unknown

On June 21st, after a rescue dig at Polis, a town north of Paphos, and the continuing work at the House of Orpheus, the team was called to a site at Westpark, which was subsequently called the 'Alexander the Great' dig, because it was beside the recently built hotel of that name. A new road was being built beside the hotel and the heavy machinery uncovered a number of tombs. It promised to be a long dig. I worked on four tombs in a row. In the first was a gold ring and scattered bones. It had been robbed and the soil was so compacted that I initially had to use a pick and shovel. Aristodemos found two more surface tombs.

The next day Sheila, Andrea and I worked on the tombs. The different strata of soil were well-defined, as I was beginning to recognise stratification of soil layers and see for myself how useful a dating tool for finds. Julianne was absent on this dig as she was enjoying a visit to Egypt.

We were all invited by the owner of a house about two hundred yards away to view the painted chamber tombs which had been excavated beneath his house. He was so proud of them. Beside his house were eucalyptus trees, a barbeque and, almost unheard of in Cyprus, a neatly clipped lawn. Usually only the Russian Mafia have lawns in Cyprus because water is scarce and expensive. It transpires that this delightful man with the Australian accent was Cypriot but had lived in England for several years, then in Australia. He loved Australia and wished to return but he wanted to stay close to family. His wife was desperate to return to Oz. I am not sure whether the lawn, gum trees and barbeque were to assuage his or his wife's longing for Australia.

Back to the graves! In the grave I was working on, the layers of soil were appearing more clearly as well as large stones and a long bronze hair pin. There were also fragments of red painted plaster and small pieces of iron. These finds did not augur well for an undisturbed tomb. The following day Demetri visited, very excited by a tomb he was excavating at Yeroskipou. This village was near to Paphos but was

Modern pottery plant pot on my wall as a reminder of Cyprus

absorbed into its larger neighbour. A bigger dig there featured prominently in my later experiences. The tomb Demetri was working on was on a hill above the town. There were eleven closed but unlooted tombs, one containing a female head sculpture in the classical tradition.

Some years later I found a pottery plant pot in a shop in Brisbane, somewhat similar but rougher, that reminded me of Demetri's exciting find. It has hung on the brick wall of the veranda behind the fireplace at my home for many years. Demetri, when visiting, commented on the coincidence.

Demetri also told me to hand a bucket to any tourist who stood watching me work for too long. One English tourist, Gordon, visited two days in a row with his five-year-old grandson and asked lots of questions. When he arrived on the third day without his grandson and asked very intelligent questions, I offered him a bucket and he spent that day and each subsequent day of his holidays emptying buckets. Such a help! Unfortunately, there were many bones but no skull or grave goods. The tomb had obviously been looted. Sheila, the English volunteer, was more fortunate. She found a gold earring in the form of a bull's head surrounded by small dots of gold. This very advanced metallurgical technique is known as granulation and was developed by Minoan craftsmen in Crete about 1500 B.C. In her tomb Sheila also found five unguentaria, one in precious blue glass. These were used for perfume or precious oils and not infrequently found in tombs as part of the grave goods. There were also more mundane sherds of red pottery.

The tomb I was working on was so long and narrow that we wondered if, in fact, it hid the steps down to the chamber tomb. Andrea reached bedrock on her grave excavation, having found a complete unguentarium (a slender vessel to collect tears of mourning), a few teeth and the remains of long bones. The excavation of these tombs was very hard work as it was unbearably hot and the soil so compacted that we had to use picks and shovels to loosen it.

Andrea's tomb yielded some beautiful jewellery. It had been a woman's resting place. There was a copper mirror lying near the head, or at least where the head would have been. The skull was never found. A simple but elegant pendant and a gold bead with granulation decorating it indicated both the wealth and good taste of the former occupant or of those who laid her to rest. A second set of earrings and a pendant in the form of a tiny pot confirmed the view that the tomb robbers had been careless – or interrupted! Of the skeleton(s) there remained only scattered long bones and a few teeth.

When the diggers joined us from the House of Orpheus, including Chrysanthos, the very short one who never missed anything, Demetri told me that they enquired whether "Pamela would be there because we miss her". I was so moved.

The tomb Sheila was working on was yielding some exciting finds. As in Andrea's tomb, a copper mirror was placed beside the head. This seems to have been a common practice in the female tombs of the period. I wonder whether it allowed the deceased to keep an eye on her toilette during the journey to the afterlife! There were two pendants. One was in the shape of a head in gold, the other a small pot. Another earring matched the style of an earlier one that was found. The skeleton was pushed to the side with the bones quite fragmented. The grave robbers had been at work yet again.

Andreas' wife (of lawn, barbeque and eucalyptus fame) came over to the dig with cold drinks, oranges and a procession of friends and children to empty buckets. Julianne returned from her Egypt trip and she and Andrea left for Australia at the end of June. I missed Julianne very much and on recent visits to me she has brought some wonderful photographs of the raising of the Orpheus Mosaic.

Towards the end of the 'Alexander the Great' dig, a volunteer from Belgium arrived. He was studying archaeology and was very enthusiastic. He and his mother had a holiday home in Paphos. I was very appreciative when they invited me to move into it, rent free, when they returned to Belgium, but I was not able to take advantage of their offer as I was soon to return to Australia. I am, however, still in touch with Marcel. He is working in the field of Prehistoric Archaeology and is married with a son. One of the delightful aspects of being an archaeologist is the camaraderie which is a feature of the profession. Of course, there are differences about the interpretation of a site, but archaeologists seem to recognise each other and when they meet, an easy friendship develops.

Andreas the archaeologist, not Andreas the home-sick Aussie, reached bedrock in the tomb he was working on. He found a complete Rhodian amphora standing upright near the entrance, a good sign for an unrobbed tomb. There was another broken amphora positioned behind the first, near the doorway. These were carried in solemn procession to the car – all that was needed was a garlanded bull!

That night we had a celebratory dinner at a restaurant under a grape arbour. It was a happy, convivial occasion and marked the end of the 'Alexander the Great' dig for me. The workmen were completing the excavation of the baths in the House of Orpheus while Anne, my English friend and I were working on the cleaning of the House itself, (but not as housemaids of course).

Chapter 13

More Cypriot hospitality

"Archaeology holds all the keys to understanding who we are and where we come from."

Sarah Pareak

After finishing on the 'Alexander the Great' dig, I enjoyed a short holiday and delved into more history across Cyprus. Helen, my Scottish friend, who lived in Paphos for the summer each year, drove me to Episkopi in a hired car. Episkopi is a small village on the way to Nicosia and not far from Petra tou Romiou. A sugar refinery which had been built by the Venetians in the Renaissance period, about the 6th Century had been excavated there recently. There are huge underground vaults, with cauldrons inside, where the sugar cane was rendered down, by boiling it. There was a large worked grinding stone, the first stage in the preparation of the cane. There were cone-shaped terracotta receptacles with holes in the top into which the liquid sugar was poured. This hardened into sugar as we know it. The residue dripped into a tray at the base, producing molasses which was fed to livestock. It is very nutritious but if it ferments it produces lactic acid poisoning which can kill the beasts. I discovered this to my cost when the vet failed to diagnose it and I lost my lovely pet donkey Violetta at home in Australia.

Helen and I became lost in searching for the sugar refinery. We asked an elderly man on the street who guided us. We were introduced to his family – twelve children, several grandchildren and some young great-grandchildren. We shared a delicious Cypriot meal and we left with homemade haloumi cheese – a delicious home delicacy. Such is the wonderful Cypriot hospitality!

On our way to Nicosia we passed through the charming old village of Kiro Kitia.

I looked forward to our visit to Nicosia, as I knew there was a lot more to see. We booked into a pleasant hotel and the next morning the Icon Museum was first on our list. The icons changed very little over several centuries. The feature most interesting to me was the fact that Mary is always depicted wearing a dark red gown whereas in the Western tradition she wears blue.

We visited the Archbishopric, a fine old building, and the Mam bookshop. This is a treasure trove of Cypriot publications and the owner is from Lebanon. She is extraordinarily knowledgeable and I emerged triumphant. By this time I had decided to study for a Master's degree on the topic of the 'Evolution of Aphrodite' so I had found a goldmine. Every time I visited there were more treasures.

Asinou church beckoned so we drove to the Troodos mountains, collected the key and were stunned as always by the imaginative illustrations. We marvelled over the joys of the virtuous in the afterlife and the rather gruesome depiction of the afterlife of the damned. The punishments for the Seven Deadly Sins feature prominently and of individuals such as Judas, which would be enough to deter anyone from sinning! On the righteous side, as well as depicting the joys of Paradise, there are well-known Biblical scenes including John the Baptist in a hair shirt, the first bath of Christ, the Raising of Lazarus and the Dormition of Mary. The church dates from different periods. The Narthex is 12th Century, the Nave 10th Century and the main body of the church dates from the 16th Century. As always, I left Asinou Church entranced by its beauty.

Another interesting village is Kakopetra which translates as 'bad rock' and derives its strange name from a story which tells of a couple 'sitting' on the rock who fall and both are killed. One wonders what they were doing while sitting, that the rock should punish them so violently. The village is in the care of the Department of Antiquities, and the steep hillside is enhanced by a permanent cold stream. In Kakopetra the houses are two-storied, with stone foundations and small stones bound with mud for the rest of the structure. One would imagine that a good deal of rebuilding needed to be done although there is not a great deal of rain in the area.

From the Troodos we drove south to Limassol giving a lift to two young soldiers along the way.

In Limassol we viewed the excavation of the baths and the Nymphaeum complex, and also the rainbow mosaic which is very beautiful. We walked down to view David Soren's excavations. The museum was closed but we met the ephor, Costas Alexandrion who offered coffee and we talked for ages about archaeology, sites and people.

He offered to open the South Gate Museum and I leapt at the chance. It was wonderful! Helen enjoyed the stories and the seismic information, (Cyprus is subject to frequent earthquakes), while I was moved by three skeletons – a man sheltering his wife and baby. It rounded off a wonderful day.

We returned to Paphos, stopping to view Petra tou Romiou.

Sarah drove Demetri and me to Amargetti where there was a shrine to Apollo Melanthos and some terracotta objects had been found. Then nearby we visited a restored monastery built on the site of a temple to Hera dating from the Ptolemaic era. An inscription was found in a smaller building. It is a stunning site and could well have been an acropolis.

We visited another monastery – the Virgin and the Golden Pomegranates. It was a beautiful, peaceful building though busy that day with baptisms and a fair. The abbot, a

Petra tou Romiou

ninety-year-old monk and a lay brother, were the only ones remaining in residence. The abbot restored icons and has also re-established the winery which is of international renown. From here we drove into the Troodos forest which is thick with walnut and plane trees, Mediterranean oaks, cypress and cedar trees. (I was interested to learn that the present 'Cedars of Lebanon' were re-introduced from Cyprus because the trees in Lebanon had all been harvested.) We had a picnic high in the mountains, with cracked walnuts which fell from a nearby tree, while fending off flies and wasps. A family of jays kept us company. (There were few birds in Cyprus because the villagers used to put lime on the branches of trees which disabled the birds so they could be captured and eaten.)

At Stavros we caught a glimpse of a Moufflon, an ancient form of sheep with short, light-brown coats. The rams have long sweeping antlers and the ewes sometimes have antlers too. The following day I visited the church of Yeroskipou. The church unusually has five domes and some elements dating from the 8th Century, such as the cross in the eastern cupola over the altar with stylised floral and geometric decoration. There were also Muslim influences with interlaced geometric design. The paintings are 10th and 11th Century which underlie 15th Century works of interest. They depict New Testament scenes such as Paul dictating to a scribe, the Birth of the Virgin, Presentation of Mary in the Temple, the Anunciation, the Birth of Christ, the Baptism of Christ and the Last Supper with Judas caught in a dramatic moment of dipping his hand in the bowl with Christ.

What an educational tour of Cyprus Helen and I enjoyed!

The day before my university friend Helen Statham arrived from Australia, I spent the day with Anne and John who lived in a delightful home overlooking Paphos. I recall that Anne was very upset when her dog Scruffy caught a hedgehog which quickly curled up and was unhurt. Anne used to feed a family of hedgehogs – delightful creatures!

There was one more event in the House of Orpheus dig before the end of my second visit to Cyprus. The team was preparing the House of Orpheus for documentary photos. I was welcomed with great enthusiasm and Helen offered help by sweeping the floor of the bath building. Sweeping the floor of a dirt floor and walls so intrigued her that it was mentioned by her son in her funeral service.

After a series of farewell dinners and lunch, Helen and I left Cyprus for Rhodes by boat on 11th September en route for Athens and Hong Kong. As Paphos and my beautiful Cyprus faded into the distance, I felt sad; but so grateful for the kindness of the people and the wonderful experiences digging!

Chapter 14

The Mosaics

"We become not a melting pot, but a beautiful mosaic. Different people, different beliefs, different yearnings, different hopes, different dreams."
Jimmy Carter

Cypriot mosaics were of particularly high quality and usually of superior craftsmanship. Mythological scenes were often preferred. Paphos, where I worked, is particularly rich in fine examples, showing the wealth in the area at that time. My favourite is the Orpheus Mosaic, which I spoke of earlier and which gives its name to the site of the "house of Orpheus". It depicts Orpheus playing his lyre and surrounded by many animals who are charmed by his music. Similar mythological scenes and mosaics have been found in many ancient sites across the region.

I gratefully defer to Demetri who provided the following description of the ancient process of laying the mosaics and their development over time.

The 'standard' method for laying the mosaics contained many variations of the following steps. The ground was prepared, which was levelled and beaten hard. The first and strongest bedding layer was the *statumen*, a conglomerate of rough stones and coarse mortar. The second layer, the *rudus*, consisted of crushed stones or gravel and pozzolana or pulverized pottery, mixed with lime mortar. The third layer was the *nucleus*, made of very fine plaster. Into the *nucleus*,

Orpheus mosaic of Paphos

while still wet, the tesserae were embedded and flattened. The mosaic surface was made more resistant by rubbing marble dust, sand and lime into it, and was further levelled with the use of emery.

The main phases in the development of mosaic pavements are as follows.

The earliest Bronze Age floors of natural stones, which are in today's Turkey, are claimed to be the 15th Century B.C. They feature a Hittite floor of triangles and curves made of shades of beige, red and black stones. The 8th Century B.C. Gordion mosaics, (also in Turkey), are the oldest decorated floor with complex geometric patterns made of small natural pebbles of different colours. The 5th Century B.C. mosaics of Olynthus, Greece, are the oldest known black and white pebble mosaics depicting mythological scenes. The 4th Century B.C. mosaics of Pella, Greece (Central Macedonia), are the best examples of multicoloured pebble mosaics with mythological scenes. Lead strips were used for defining colours. The 3rd Century B.C. mosaics of Morgantina, Sicily, are the earliest known mosaics made of tesserae, the most famous of which depicts the Rape of Ganymede. Tesserae are specially cut cubes of stone that increased the colour palette and became the standard way of making mosaics. A bit later, other materials, glass in particular, were also used in order to enhance the colours and make mosaics more like paintings in stone.

Chapter 15

A short winter visit to Cyprus

"Never throw in the trowel."
An Archaeological Miscellany

I returned to Cyprus several times between 1990 and 2004. In December 1990 I visited for a short Christmas visit. Because of the cold weather it was unlikely we would be excavating unless any rescue digs appeared. By this time, however, I was studying for my Master of Arts degree. Much of my research was carried out at CAARI, the Cyprus American Archaeological Research Institute. It has a very well-resourced library and a knowledgeable, friendly staff. Occasionally I worked in the University of Cyprus Library but the female librarian was both crotchety and unhelpful.

On Christmas Day, my Scottish friend Helen and I spent the day together, climbing the coastal cliffs like mountain goats and lunching at a taverna.

I was living at the home of Sarah and Demetri and looking after the children. Their parents were in England awaiting the birth of their daughter Pamela. All their children were born in the U.K. because of the disturbed political situation in Cyprus. By being born in the U.K. they had British citizenship. I remember my embarrassment when, unused to three ebullient boys, I burnt Sarah's nice saucepan beyond redemption. School had resumed. Alexi, the second son, about seven years of age, was very ill all night. He was unable to do his homework. He was obviously terrified to face his teacher so I went with Alexi to explain. She would not believe me and was so rude and spoke quite angrily to Alexi. I was horrified that such an unsympathetic character was in charge of children, especially young children.

After the birth of Pamela and a memorable winter visit to Cyprus, I returned home again to Brisbane, to my regular life of teaching at a girls' school and looking after my myriad animals - donkeys, goats, a pig, hens, dogs and cats. I felt like Orpheus surrounded by animals, so the ancient world was never far away.

Every trench tells a story

Chapter 16

Stories amongst the sherds

> *"What woman, having ten silver coins, if she loses one of them, does not light a lamp, sweeps the house, and search carefully until she finds it? And when she has found it, she calls her friends and neighbours together, saying, 'rejoice with me, for I have found the piece which I lost!!'"*
>
> Luke 15: 8-10

It did not seem long before I returned to Cyprus, in June 1992. Excavation work was still in progress at the House of Orpheus. I was working with the team cleaning the floors and opening new rooms enabling the area to be dated. There was a lot of wall plaster – red, gold and black, which was probably Fourth Style. I was excited to find my first coin of the Hellenistic period. I was pleased to discover that my knack of matching and joining sherds of pottery had not abandoned me! This time it was an amphora. The workmen discovered a small shrine in situ, surrounded by a temenos of stones. The shrine was in a form of an upturned cippus. Demetri hoped it was a shrine to Arsinoe, a Ptolemaic queen, who became a household deity during the Hellenistic period, but he felt it was probably from a later period.

After lunch I cleaned out a large, partly broken amphora which Neoptolemus had dived for near the harbour. It was full of sand, stones and seaweed but nothing else. Disappointing!

Costas, Demetri's eldest son, had broken his arm the day before I arrived and it was in traction. Demetri was obviously very worried but Costas was to recover well. After work, I went in search of a gift for Costas. My preference was for a kaleidoscope, but none was available so I bought some dominoes instead. Then Neoptolemus drove us to the hospital which was quite an impressive building – but it leaked! Nevertheless, it smelled and looked like a hospital anywhere.

Costas' arm looked very sore, but he was very brave though obviously uncomfortable.

The following day the heat was oppressive so we abandoned work until the cooler part of the afternoon. The workmen were removing the baulks and in it was found a tiny terracotta hot water bottle, suitable either for a baby or a finger! A complete set of terracotta hot water bottles was found in a doctor's tomb and is displayed in the Paphos Museum.

Hot water bottle found

Where's My Bucket and Spade?

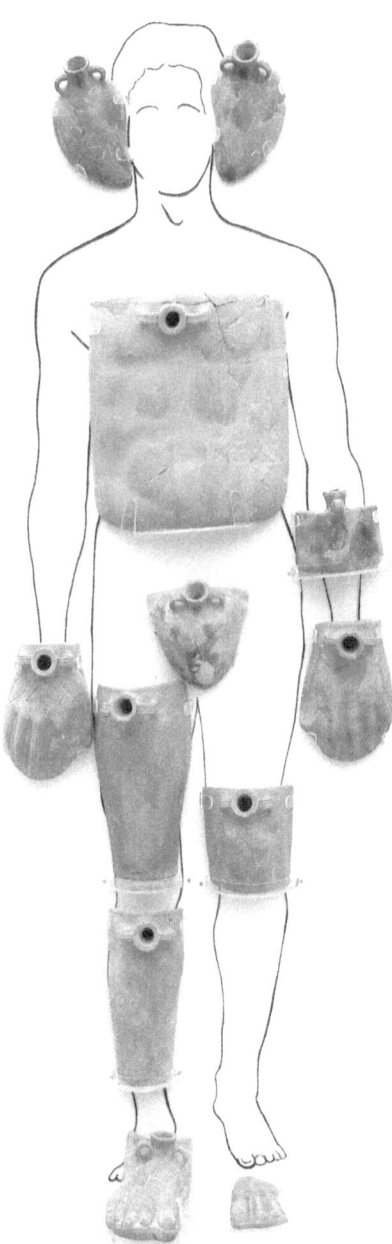

Hot water bottles,
Paphos Museum

The following day, while I spent time putting pottery together before going over to the trench to continue clearing the wall, the workmen found some very interesting objects. More fragments of the hot water bottle were found, of a shape suitable for a foot. Also found were lamp fragments in terracotta and perforated with holes. The base and top were missing but most of the body was redeemable. Several complete, small lamps also were found and the breast and one arm of a small faience statue from Egypt.

Apparently that trench had held a number of hot water bottle fragments, as well as large storage amphora and Agora ware amphora (with one handle). There was also a broken pestle in marble and finally, a rock crystal earring with a tear-drop shaped stone attached to copper wire – a lovely little thing for which there must have been much searching. The other trench, with the 'shrine', is still a great puzzle to Demetri. Lots of large, worked stones – one of them in the shape of an open drain. A drain – the basis of civilisation!

As we prepared the area for photography Demetri decided to remove a number of re-used capitals from a small room of unknown purpose. It was, as always, a dramatic occasion as the men 'man-handled' the heavy blocks out of the trench with ropes and boards. They were made from local sandstone, extremely weathered! Two were pilasters and one the capital of a round column. In style, they were debased Corinthian, the round one appeared to be Hadrianic with the clusters of leaves on the corners. One pilaster was so badly worn as to be impossible to reconstruct, the other one more complete.

The following day, quite a number of interesting sherds were discovered, including an attractive piece of Cypriot sigillata. Also discovered was a small, copper stud – about the size of a ten-cent piece – which probably decorated a piece of furniture. In the trench next to ours, under the area from which the capitals had been removed, a small cooking pot was found with the lid in place. It stood on the floor in the corner, obviously placed there on purpose.

It was a moving find – who had put it there? Why had it not been recovered? Why was it on the floor? What was in it? Chrysanthos, digging in his usual neat, spare manner, found a complete, small unguentaria which Demetri said he had never seen the shape of before. It was much larger and more capacious than most. There were also some complete fragments of Roman amphoras.

The day ended with a lavish Cypriot meal and an 'archaeologist's smile' – a badly sunburnt back – where my shirt and shorts had parted company!

On one occasion, my English friend Anne and I took part in an unproductive dig. The workmen had exposed a large drain which appeared to be the main drain from Kato Paphos. When Demetri asked them to dig back into the drain, they refused fearing it would collapse. Anne and I accepted the challenge believing that after 2000 years it would probably be safe. We donned our yellow hard hats (which would have provided little protection had the drain collapsed). Taking it in turns we were able to go back 10 metres finding only tiny sherds. What had we hoped to find? Earrings? A ring slipped down with the washing-up water? A false tooth? A coin?

Pamela and Anne digging in a drain, Kato Paphos
Original illustration © Geoff Ginn

Chapter 17

Yeroskipou, Aphrodite's sacred gardens

"Beautiful out of the sea-deeps cold Aphrodite arose—the Flower of Time—"
                                          Victor James Daley

On one visit, I was working with Demetri in the House of Orpheus when we received an invitation to dig in the municipality of Yeroskipou – a bulldozer had uncovered a site and the municipality asked us to clear it. The town of Yeroskipou had largely merged with Kato Paphos. Demetri's students went home at weekends, leaving an American couple who were Presbyterian ministers in training. Terrified to be left alone in the dig house, the husband confessed he slept with a handgun under his pillow. I commented that I slept with a handkerchief under mine! I was sad to see such fear, as Cyprus was such a safe place really.

The Yeroskipou municipality had given us luxurious accommodation in a motel – a big change from the dig house. We were in the lap of luxury and were served with delicious meals. At Yeroskipou, the bulldozers building the road uncovered some ruins, which when cleaned revealed the remains of a burial church. It was very exciting indeed because the Byzantine church had paving but over each tomb there was a mosaic. Greek mosaic specialists were called to lift the mosaics from over the tombs.

Mosaic floor and tomb exposed

At the end of one day, we found a stone-lined tomb which contained a female skeleton. She wore extensive jewellery and a gown with maroon silk, threaded through with gold. When the forensic archaeologist examined her body, she was found to be in her forties and was suffering pre-mortem tooth loss, scoliosis and osteoporosis. Wealthy she may have been, but her later years must have been very painful.

There was a baulk which contained hundreds of roof tiles, very rough on my hands, which were bleeding by this stage after scrubbing and digging. Demetri looked hopefully at me and said, "These tiles need to be cleaned and investigated, Pam." My response was, "Demetri, if I never see another tile, it will be too soon!" This was the first request I had declined Demetri in all my years working with him.

While digging at the House of Orpheus, we unexpectedly found a burial along the line of a foundation wall with a tombstone horizontal above it. Demetri thought it must be Arab because it was found inside the wall, therefore it was

Two views at Yeroskipou, showing uncovering of skeletons - original illustrations © Geoff Ginn

not pagan; there was no church nearby, therefore it was not Christian. This is the only area known to have Arab burials.

Beside it was a wall plastered with hydraulic plaster and a low wall with moulding in the same plaster – obviously to contain water – was it a fishpond for takeaway? The amphitheatre was nearby. Demetri thought that we might have been in the public baths since no baths have been identified except those in the House of Orpheus, which were open to the public as well as the household.

We were all exhausted and as red as turkey cocks, but moved the stones very efficiently using a bucket brigade. Great fun, perhaps we should have broken into the Volga Boat Song.

I returned home via Athens. A member of a Greek/Australian football team asked me where I had been. "Cyprus," I replied. His comment was, "Oh, we own that!" I looked at him with my best school-teacherly glare and

Sometimes a hard hat is required!

Its hot work under the Cypriot sun

replied, "Indeed you don't, it is an independent Republic within the British Commonwealth!" and then he added a feeble, "Ooh."

The ancient world continued to beckon. Over several years, I organised and led tours of Greece and Turkey, Italy, Portugal, Spain, Morocco, Tunesia, Iran, Syria and Lebanon for past parents and students of the girls' school where I taught Ancient History. A series of workshops preceded each tour for the enthusiastic participants. The tours were well attended and I enjoyed them immensely.

As I finish my story, it is time to part with my beloved Cyprus. Once while sitting on the plane, my thoughts returned to my times digging and travelling and all the wonderful experiences I had had in Cyprus. My memory returned to a moment when I had stood in Yeroskipou, which means 'holy garden' or 'sacred garden' in Greek, and is the place where Aphrodite had her gardens in Greek mythology.

Amongst these ruins that hid timeless stories, I felt my own story encircle me. With the passing of my mother, I was alone in the world, except for the ancient history that unfolded at each ancient site.

Cyprus Sunset

Illustrations

Original illustrations by Geoff Ginn

Chapter 2
Figures 1 and 2 – Maps, showing the geographical position of Cyprus and a map of the island, illustrating the major towns
Figure 3 – Botticelli's *Birth of Venus*

Chapter 3
Figure 4 – Mending pottery under the eucalyptus tree
Figure 5 – So many pottery sherds!
Figures 6 and 7 – Amphora: cross section of ship's hull showing the storage pattern of amphorae in transit; kiln design and stacking arrangement for making amphorae
Figure 8 – Three amphorae in stands
Figures 9, 10 and 11 – Stamped handles of amphorae

Chapter 5
Figure 12 – Diggers on site, Kyriakou and Chrysanthos
Figure 13 – My sitting down style of digging

Chapter 7
Figure 14 – The theatre at Palmyra, Syria

Chapter 8
Figure 15 – The tombs of the kings site
Figure 16 – Saranda Kolones site
Figures 17 and 18 – Kourion site and the theatre

Chapter 9
Figure 19 – The Church of Panagia of Asinou
Figure 20 – Detail of one of the many frescoes

Chapter 11
Figure 21 – Aristodemos digging in the cesspit
Figure 22 – Demetri at the House of Orpheus
Figure 23 – The audience watching the mosaic being moved
Figure 24 – Mosaic on the wooden roller and the big crane
Figure 25 – Mosaic being carefully lifted in the air
Figure 26 – Mosaic being lifted back to its original location, with a new concrete base
Figure 27 – Buongiorno Orfeo! The mosaic revealed, the water shows the brilliant colours
Figure 28 – TV crew filming the reveal of the restored mosaic
Figure 29 – Detail of Orpheus from the mosaic

Chapter 12
Figure 30 – Modern pottery plant pot on the wall

Chapter 13
Figure 31 – Petra tou Romiou

Chapter 14
Figure 32 – Orpheus mosaic of Paphos (Getty Conservation Institute)

Chapter 15
Figure 33 – Every trench tells a story

Chapter 16
Figure 34 – Hot water bottle found
Figure 35 – Hot water bottles in Paphos Museum
Figure 36 – Pamela and Anne digging in drain, Kato Paphos

Chapter 17
Figure 37 – Yeroskipou mosaic floor and tomb exposed
Figures 38 and 39 – Two views at Yeroskipou,
    showing the uncovering of skeletons
Figure 40 – Sometimes a hard hat is required!
Figure 41 – Its hot work under the Cypriot sun
Figure 42 – Sunset

www.ingramcontent.com/pod-product-compliance
Lightning Source LLC
Chambersburg PA
CBHW032047290426
44110CB00012B/990